YOUR MONEY IS NOT FOR THE GRAVE

Get Through Life's Most Difficult Time Without Losing Your Mind or Your Money

Lori Hadley Davis

ILLUMINATION PRESS
Atlanta, Georgia

YOUR MONEY IS NOT FOR THE GRAVE
Get Through Life's Most Difficult Time Without Losing Your Mind or Money

Copyright © 2018 by Lori Hadley Davis

All rights reserved. No part of this publication may be reproduced or transmitted in any form or by any means, including informational storage and retrieval systems, without permission in writing from the copyright holder, except for brief quotations in a review and certain other noncommercial uses permitted by copyright law.

ISBN: 978-1-7322384-5-9

Cover and Interior Design by AugustPride, LLC
Photography by Al Freddy

ILLUMINATION PRESS
1100 Peachtree Street, Suite 250
Atlanta, Georgia 30309
United States

Contact the Author: Bless GodLoi@yahoo.com

Contents

Introduction	01
My Story	09
How To Use This Book	17
Part I: Be Ye Ready	19
Having The Difficult Conversations	21
Considering Insurance	31
Watch Out!	37
Building Lasting Memories	47
Part 2: The Homegoing Celebration	53
First Things First	55
Choosing The Right Funeral Home	63
Meeting With The Funeral Director	71
Funeral Etiquette	79
What's Next?	85
Words of Comfort & Encouragement	95
About The Author	103
Notes	107

Introduction

I have been called by God to serve.

Blessed way more than I deserve.

Protected and cherished by the Lord above

Filled with His grace, mercy, and holy love.

Into a divine calling I've been thrust

I will be obedient and forever trust

He gave me this gift for a special reason

That I might serve in every season.

As long as I'm here on this Earth living

I'll keep helping, praying, loving, and giving.

~Lori Hadley Davis

When people ask me why I got into the funeral business, my only response is—It's my calling. I didn't choose the funeral business. It chose me. I truly believe God created me for this special purpose.

From a very early age, I've always been fascinated by dead people. Not in a morbid or

gruesome way - I am not into dark or spooky things. My interest in dead people goes much deeper to a spiritual place.

    I view my service as a special part of God's work transitioning His children from their earthly residences to their Heavenly home. It's an honor to me and something I take very seriously. That's why owning a funeral home and being a licensed funeral director is more than just a business to me. It's my ministry. It's how I honor and serve not just the people who come into the doors of Hadley Davis, it is how I honor and serve God.

    That's why I am so passionate about upholding the standards of excellence and compassion within the funeral industry. It is also why I am writing this book.

The Funeral Industry is Deteriorating

    Over the past decade or so, I have seen

a drastic decline in the quality and caliber of service within the funeral industry. So many people these days are getting into the funeral business for the wrong reasons. They don't care about people. They don't care about the professional standards. The only thing that matters to them is adding to the zeros at the end of their bank account.

  People looking to make a quick buck will open up a funeral home as a type of get rich quick scheme. They don't have the proper education or training. They don't have any experience in the funeral industry. They don't even have a passion for it. All they see is dollar signs.

  As a result, their funeral homes open today, and, in a few short months, they are out of business. If somehow, they do manage to stay in business, they hold on by offering extremely low prices to undercut other funeral homes. People

are drawn to these funeral homes because of the prices but are disappointed when they receive inferior, low quality services and their loved ones aren't treated with the proper care and honor they deserve.

You Must Be Educated

What really makes me mad is that these pop-up funeral homes are predominately in poor African American communities. People who are already struggling with very few resources are being swindled out of their insurance money.

There once was a time when the funeral home owner and the funeral home director were the same person. As a licensed funeral director, the funeral home owner was educated and had a degree. They received intensive training and were required to go through a process of apprenticeship and internship in the industry according to the state licensing requirements.

Because the funeral home owner was a licensed funeral director, he or she was committed to upholding the standards of integrity in the industry and abide by the laws governing our licensure. There was a connection, a passion, and a purpose behind the funeral home business.

Today, most funeral home owners are not licensed funeral directors. They have not been educated or trained. The most experience they have in the industry is attending a funeral or maybe hanging around a funeral home to check out the processes. Some of them even get to a point where they think they know more than the licensed funeral director, but they won't (or can't) go to college and pass the licensing test. They don't know any of the standards and they definitely don't understand the passion and purpose of the funeral industry. What usually happens is that they decide a funeral home is a great business to start and they find a licensed

funeral director is no longer working in the industry or has a full-time job somewhere else The business owner will then pay the licensed funeral director a monthly fee to use his or her license. This trend has been so detrimental to the funeral industry that some states are now requiring both funeral home directors and funeral home owners to be educated and licensed. Prayerfully, all states will get on board with this requirement.

Another trend that is very disturbing to me is the trend of clergy members becoming involved in the funeral home business. They either partner with established funeral homes and request a referral kickback for each member they send to the funeral home or they open their own funeral home and "buy the license" of a funeral director. It is a trend that capitalizes on their position as a spiritual leader. Instead

of guiding their grieving members through the process of spiritual healing after losing a loved one, they are being guided by a profit motive. Now, please don't get me wrong. All ministers and pastors are not following this trend. However, I have seen enough of it to know that it is prevalent in our communities.

You might be thinking, "Aren't there associations that make sure this kind of thing doesn't happen?" The answer is yes…and no.

The Morticians Association is a professional organization for funeral home directors and funeral home owners. Its purpose is to provide support and resources for the funeral home owners and directors to help them better serve the community. Each state also has a licensing board to guard against any wrong doing in the industry. Most of the associations however have become cliques. They are little more than social

clubs. The barriers to entry are oftentimes how much money you are making and the types of cars you are driving. If the members like you, you get in. If they don't like you, you are blackballed. Instead of protecting the community they are protecting the unscrupulous practices that have been tearing the funeral home industry apart.

Again, I must say—not all associations and association members are in this category. I am making a comment on the trends I am seeing that are harmful to the funeral industry as a whole. Most likely, those who are acting in integrity will not have a problem with the information I am sharing, and they will applaud me for being courageous enough to speak out against the wrong doing. It is only those who are being exposed that will have an issue. As the old folks used to say, "a hit dog will holler."

As I mentioned before, I take very seriously my calling to serve people and guide them through the challenges of dealing with dying, death, and bereavement. My heart is for the people. It is my hope that as you read this book, you will gain a deeper understanding of what the funeral process entails so that you will be empowered and equipped to make the right decisions—financially and emotionally.

My Story

There is nothing worse than getting advice from someone who has no idea what they are talking about. That's why it's important that you know I have the background, education, and heart to help you. Once you read just a little bit about my story, you'll know that you can trust me to guide you in the right direction.

So here we go…

My love for the funeral business began as a young girl. I have always loved dead people and found it quite fascinating to hear my mother tell me about her job working in a family member's funeral home. Whereas most young children would find this dreadful, I found it captivating. I always wanted to learn more and more.

I dreamed about one day being able to work in a funeral home and, maybe if I was blessed enough, I would have my own. As early as age nine, I started to act out my dreams. I took it so far that I would often play a game called Funeral with my twin sister and other friends from my neighborhood. You've probably never heard of this game before because it is one that I made up.

I would be the funeral director and give the eulogies. My sister and friends would alternate roles. Someone would be the dead

body and others would be the grieving family members. I don't know about them, but I had the time of my life playing Funeral. The game was more than just fun to me. Even back then I knew I had a special place in my heart for people who were transitioning to be with the Lord.

As I grew up and held various jobs and had various businesses, the desire to get into the funeral industry was always there. When I opened up Lori's Gifted Hands, my hair salon, I would work at night in a funeral home styling hair and preparing the deceased for their homegoing celebrations.

After expressing my interest to a friend over and over again, I was encouraged to go back to school to get a degree and become a licensed funeral director.

The process of getting my degree was grueling but I found it worth the sacrifice of long

days working in my hair salon and late nights studying while still maintaining my role as a wife and mother of three young children.

Once I earned my degree and passed the test to become a licensed funeral director I was excited to finally be able to live my dreams. But, the challenge was just beginning.

In my book, Faith Through It All, I share my experiences of setback and struggle as I fought my way through all of the obstacles and roadblocks that tried to prevent me from getting into the funeral business. Being rejected… blackballed and shunned by other funeral home owners in the area…shut out of the Morticians Association…having major issues in my first funeral home… All of these things worked against me as I attempted to do what I knew God had called me to do.

But, I know that anything worth having has its price, not just financially but also in effort and sometimes even obstacles and challenges. Through all of this—the victories and the defeats—my God causes all things to work together for the good of them who love Him and are called according to His purpose!

I have held on to the truth of Romans 8:28 through all of the ups and downs. I love God and I am indeed called according to His purpose.

That's why, when I opened Hadley Davis Funeral Home in 2009, I was committed to upholding the highest standard of quality and excellence. I wanted to bring the dignity and distinction I knew the funeral industry needed. My vision is to bring elegant and professional services at an affordable price.

    I opened up Hadley Davis to be a beacon of light and hope in the community. Each and every person who walks through the doors of Hadley Davis becomes a part of our family—and, family means the world to me. I make sure my family is taken care of and I don't let anyone hurt or harm them. And, now that you are reading this book, you have become a part of the extended Hadley Davis family. Whether you come to Hadley Davis or receive services from any other funeral home, my desire is for you to be educated and empowered with truth and understanding.

    Read this book knowing I have nothing but your best interest in mind. I want to educate and empower you to make the right decisions during what can be the most difficult time of a person's life.

How to use this book

Your Money Is Not For The Grave is a practical guide to help you prepare for and deal with one of the most difficult times of your life—the death and bereavement of a loved one. This book is not just about helping you navigate through the complicated and confusing process of planning and orchestrating the homegoing of a loved one. I want to give you honest and heartfelt advice about handling the emotional, mental, and financial hardships that dying and death can bring.

I have written this book in two parts:

- Part I—Be Ye Ready—helps you to understand what to do before a loved one dies. Having the difficult conversations and planning for the financial and emotional

challenges of death can ease the overwhelm and frustration of having to deal with it during the grieving process.

- Part II—The Homegoing Celebration—gives you everything you need to know about planning a loved one's celebration of life service. From meeting with the funeral director to planning the service, this section will help you to take the guesswork out of the process.

I know how important comforting words can be during a difficult time, so I have shared some powerful wisdom to encourage, inspire, and uplift you. At the end of the book, you will find a Notes section to help you keep track of your plans and have all of your important details in one handy place. This isn't a book you will read just once and put on a shelf. My prayer is that you will use it as a resource guide to help make the process easier for you.

PART I
Be Ye Ready

"So, you also must be ready, for the Son of Man will come at an hour when you do not expect Him."

Matthew 24:44

Having The Difficult Conversations

> *"Get ready; be prepared, you and all the hosts around you."*
> Ezekiel 38:7

Life is too short.

Most people don't like to talk about it, but it's true. None of us will live forever. We are only here on this earth for a limited time and these days it seems as if that life span is getting shorter and shorter.

There was a time when most of the funerals I would do were funerals of older people—grandmothers and grandfathers who had lived long lives. Although very painful and

heartbreaking, their deaths were somewhat expected and anticipated at their advanced ages.

But, times have shifted. I see thirty-year olds who have died from heart attacks…teenagers killed by senseless gun violence…people killing for nonsense…new mothers falling prey to domestic violence…fathers taken away from their families with senseless brutality—all of these young people in the prime of their lives taken away before they even had a chance to fully live.

When the families come in to the funeral home they are distraught and devastated. Caught up in the grief and pain of their loved one's death, they can barely think straight let alone have the mental energy to plan and prepare for their loved one's homegoing.

That's why it's so important that we have these types of discussions. You might not be able

to predict the time of your death, but you can certainly prepare for it.

When we AVOID difficult conversations we trade short term discomfort for long term dysfunction.

One of the most challenging aspects of my role as a funeral director is to help a grieving family navigate all of the decisions that must be made while planning a loved one's homegoing celebration. When people are mourning it is very difficult for them to think about anything but their sorrow. Their hearts are hurting, and they have to push it aside to deal with all of the complications of planning a funeral.

That's why I strongly suggest you talk to your loved ones and find out how they

would want their services to be. And, don't just ask your loved ones about their wishes. Make sure you let your family members know your wishes, too.

Now I know—conversations about death can be tough. Things like planning a funeral service or body disposition is morbid but it is crucial. Talking about it in advance can give you and your loved ones a sense of control over your destiny and legacy.

How To Start The Conversation

I know everyone is not like me. I have no problem discussing death and dying. Most people, however, put off the discussion until they have to deal with it.

The best way to bring up the subject is in normal conversation. It doesn't have to be a

special occasion or a family meeting—just bring it up while discussing things happening in the world. With all of the things going on in the world lately, there are plenty of opportunities to bring up the subject.

    For instance, the recent natural disasters and random acts of violence are ways to lead into the conversation.

    Say, for example you heard about a young man who left home one day and never returned. You could start off the conversation in this way—

    "Did you see the news about that young man who just died? Wasn't that a tragic thing? I wonder how his family is dealing with that loss. There is a lot that has to go into taking care of someone once they pass away. I often think about what would happen when I die, and I don't want you all to have to stress over how to plan my funeral."

The first reaction your family members will probably have is, "what's wrong?" They will automatically assume you are ill. Reassure them that nothing is wrong. Let them know you are not trying to upset them. You only want to discuss it because you see all of the tragedies going on and we never know what will happen in life from day to day. Tell them, "I don't want you to be burdened about having to make difficult decisions about my final expenses and funeral service while you are grieving."

Make Your Wishes Known

Tell your loved ones what you would want after you die. For instance…

- Do you want to be buried in a casket or cremated?

- Do you want a traditional church service or a small family gathering?

- Have you thought about the funeral home you want to use?
- What kind of music and flowers do you want at your service?
- Who would you like to speak at your service?
- Who would you like to be the pall bearers?
- What scriptures or inspirational passages would you like to be read?
- Have you picked out a cemetery?
- Do you have any insurance policies or final expense plans?
- Do you have a will? If not, who do you want to get your valuables?

There are lots of other questions you can answer, but these will get the ball rolling. The main thing you want to do is to share your wishes with the ones you love. This way they will know exactly what you want instead of trying to guess about it after you're gone.

Encourage Your Loved Ones To Discuss Their Wishes

While you are sharing your wishes with your loved ones, encourage your loved ones to share their wishes with you.

The time to discuss these things is while your loved ones are in good health. If your loved one is terminally ill or close to death, it can be extremely stressful to determine what they want for their final arrangements.

If a direct approach won't work because it is too upsetting for you or your loved ones, try to bring up the subject in casual conversation. Remind them that you want to make sure they have a proper and dignified service that honors them to the fullest.

Having the Difficult Conversations
CHECKLIST

Whether you are discussing your wishes or the wishes of your loved ones, here are some of the details you will want to include:

Body Disposition (burial or cremation)

- If you choose burial, where you wish to be buried and any details of any cemetery plot, lot, or crypt you may have purchased. (Also include the original paperwork) You should also indicate whether you want to be embalmed or not

- If you choose cremation, what you would like done with your cremation remains (e.g. scattered at a certain location, kept in the family home, interned in a mausoleum)

The type of ceremony you wish to have (e.g. traditional church service, informal

celebration of life service, memorial service at the funeral home, etc.)

- Payment for your body disposition and funeral or memorial service. You may have prepaid for your funeral, or you may have purchased a life insurance policy that should cover these costs. Make a note of any details in your checklist and include all of your original paperwork for any prepaid funeral plan or insurance policy.

If you wish, your checklist could also include details about your preferences with regard to:

- The funeral home
- Pallbearers
- Speakers giving the eulogy
- Music played and sung at your service
- Types of flowers
- Your favorite charities (if people want to make a donation in your name)

Considering Insurance

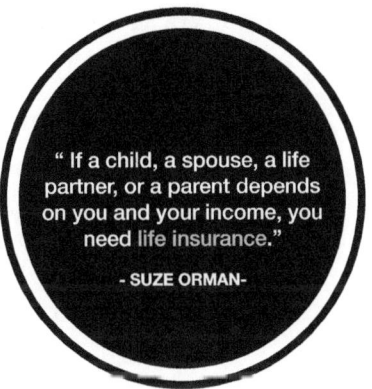

" If a child, a spouse, a life partner, or a parent depends on you and your income, you need life insurance."

- SUZE ORMAN-

Have you ever known a family whose loved one died without life insurance and the family could not afford the burial expenses?

I certainly have—I see it all the time. It's a heart wrenching thing to witness.

More times than I would like to remember, I've seen families already wrecked with grief torn apart even further when they had to face the frustration that comes when they don't have

enough money to cover their loved one's funeral expenses.

    Most people know they need life insurance. The problem is, they just cannot afford it. These days even people who have good jobs struggle to find the money to pay monthly life insurance premiums. In the African American and other minority communities life insurance is a luxury they cannot afford. And, for those that can somehow afford it, there are pre-existing conditions that prevent them from qualifying for life insurance at reasonable rates. I, too, have faced this challenge. When I went to purchase a life insurance policy for my family, I was denied at first because of high blood pressure. I did research and shopped around but most insurance companies would not cover me and the ones who would wanted to charge extremely high premiums. It took a while for me to find insurance coverage that was not sky high.

I did the research, but it took quite some time. Most people won't go that far. They don't have the time or resources to spend trying to search for the right life insurance policy. What ends up happening is they give up and decide to just let their loved ones figure it all out once they are gone. That is not the most ideal way to handle it, but it's the reality of what happens most times.

Can You Afford To Die?

At the end of their lives, many people, quite literally, cannot afford to die.

At the time I am writing this, the average cost of a basic funeral is $6,000. which includes things like embalming and preparing your loved one for the funeral service, viewing and service, hearse, and transfer of remains. In my opinion, the average funeral price is high, and I believe funeral prices should be much more affordable.

After all, the $6,000 price for the basic funeral does not include other things like the repass or cemetery fees. It also doesn't cover expenses such as legal fees, medical bills, and credit card debt your loved one may leave behind.

Dying Without Insurance Can Be Devastating

There aren't a lot of people who have tens of thousands of dollars just lying around. It's hard to come up with that kind of money—especially when something unexpected happens.

If you die without life insurance to cover your final expenses and your family can't afford to pay for your funeral, your survivors may have to come up with alternative measures. They might have to get a loan, start a fundraising campaign, or resorting to do something they don't want to do.

Choosing Life Insurance

Now that you realize how important it is for you to have life insurance, I hope your next step is to make sure you have enough coverage to take care of your final expenses. I also want to make sure you have the right kind of life insurance and that you are not overpaying.

My advice to you--do your homework. You don't have to choose the first insurance company you find out about.

Here are some questions you'll want to ask:

- How long has the company been around? What is the company's track record?
- What policy options are available?
- Does the policy provide cash value?
- What is guaranteed in the policy?
- Does the policy change if your health changes?

- Will the death benefit be adjusted for inflation?
- What happens if I become disabled or can't pay the premium?
- What happens as I age?
- How quickly does the company pay out benefits?

Watch Out!

BEWARE, SOME PEOPLE WILL SELL YOU A DREAM AND DELIVER A NIGHTMARE.

During my tenure of serving the community, I have seen so many funeral homes pop up. They are here today and gone tomorrow. Uneducated, unlicensed individuals

are opening up funeral homes solely for the financial gain. They do not have the best interest of the grieving families at heart. I'm going to talk a lot about this when I help you plan for the funeral service in Part II, however, I think it's something I should mention here as well because the scams don't just start when a loved one dies. They happen to well-meaning people who are trying to take care of their families before they die.

When I purchased the building for Hadley Davis' second location, I bought a space previously owned by another funeral home that had gone out of business many years before. Not too long after we opened that location, an elderly woman came in. She had purchased a pre-needs policy from the owners of the previous funeral home for several thousands of dollars. She was coming in to make sure

everything was in order.

It broke my heart to tell this woman that there was nothing we could do. Although we purchased the building, we had no connection to the previous funeral home. When that funeral home went out of business, this woman, and all the countless others who had purchased pre-needs policies directly from that funeral home, lost all the money they paid.

Unfortunately, this is not a rare occurrence. Thousands upon thousands of people every day are scammed by shiesty funeral homes that don't stay in business long enough to perform the services for which people have already paid. That's why I don't recommend anyone getting a pre-needs policy for themselves or a loved one and paying money directly to the funeral home.

Just so you will know why I don't recommend

pre-needs, let me break it down a bit so you can understand.

A pre-needs policy pays for the costs of a funeral service and burial or cremation. What is unusual about a pre-needs policy compared to other types of life insurance is you are working directly with a funeral home. The funeral home will first look at the expenses you will likely have to pay for your funeral. Those are the expenses that will be covered by your pre-needs policy.

Another unusual thing about a pre-needs policy is that the beneficiary of a pre-needs policy is the funeral home. They'll get the money directly to pay for their services.

The Good

The good thing about a pre-needs policy is that it takes the guesswork out of the funeral services decision-making process. There are so many decisions to make when planning a funeral

service. For a family already grieving those decisions can be overwhelming.

When you work with a funeral home ahead of time to settle on what you want, the pre-needs policy pays for those costs and there's not much else to handle. That can make it easier on your loved ones. With that being said, there are a lot of bad consequences to purchasing a pre-needs policy. For most people these bad consequences far outweigh any benefit.

The Bad

The first bad thing about a pre-needs policy is that it is very limited. You are paying directly to the funeral home. Some policies are specific to that funeral home and most of them cannot be transferred to another funeral home. Your loved ones have no flexibility with the benefit.

Another drawback of a pre-needs policy

is that it will tie up money for a long time if you end up living longer than you thought. In many cases, you'd be better off investing the money and leaving it to your loved ones.

    Something you might also want to consider is there's a period of time when your policy may not be fully matured. There is a contestability period determined by your policy and during this time the benefit from your policy is reduced. If you die before your policy matures, you won't get the full face value of your policy and your loved ones will have to cover the difference.

    Your loved ones may also have to pay extra money if the price for the services goes up. If your policy doesn't cover a flat amount, your family could be out of thousands of more dollars to pay for your funeral.

A Good Alternative To Pre-Needs

Final expense insurance can be an alternative to a pre-needs policy.

The difference between a pre-needs policy and final expense insurance is that while pre-need is paid directly to the funeral home for a pre-determined amount, final expense insurance works like any other kind of insurance type. Final expense insurance is not directly tied to a particular funeral home.

Your family gets the death benefit and can use it to pay for funeral expenses, but it's not tied to that. They can also use the benefit to pay for any last medical expenses or post-funeral expenses.

Don't Forget The Cemetery

Please be careful. When purchasing a cemetery plot, make sure everything is

included—the plot, the opening and closing, the vault, and the headstone. In most cases, when people purchase they are not sold all the things they need for a burial and end up having to pay even more money in the end.

Just as you make careful preparations for your loved one's final wishes for the homegoing celebration, also take the time to decide on and set aside money for the cemetery.

When selecting your cemetery make sure you pay close attention to all of the details. Many cemeteries also own funeral homes and they will try to bundle the cemetery with the funeral services with inflated prices. You don't have to use the cemetery's funeral home. In most cases your funeral will be more affordable if you choose a funeral home not connected with the cemetery.

I maintain my previous warning against

a pre-needs policy for the funeral home. However, when it comes to the cemetery, I highly recommend it.

In the African American community, there are not many choices for cemeteries

As demand for burial plots increase drastically, so do the burial prices. Over the past ten years I have seen the price of cemetery plots almost double. Having a pre-needs policy will ensure that you lock in your burial price. Unlike funeral home pre-needs policies, however, you won't have to worry about the cemetery going out of business. Your cemetery pre-needs policy stays with the land.

Building Lasting Memories

THE BEST GIFTS IN THE WORLD ARE NOT IN THE MATERIAL OBJECTS ONE CAN BUY FROM THE STORE, BUT IN THE MEMORIES WE MAKE WITH THE PEOPLE WE LOVE.

— Amanda Boyarshinov

What legacy will you leave behind?

We've talked a lot already about the financial matters—making sure your loved ones are able to handle the costs of final expenses and are also able to live securely after the funeral. However, creating a legacy is more than just about money.

Your legacy is made up of all the pieces of yourself that others will remember you by. It could be momentous like a recipe, a picture, a diary, or family heirloom. It could also be memories like a family vacation, a conversation, or a touching moment shared. Big or small, this is the legacy that will far outlast any amount of money.

One of the biggest regrets a person will have after their loved one has passed is that they didn't spend enough time with them… that they

didn't get to say all the things they wanted to say…that they didn't get to have that last hug or kiss…that they didn't get to hear all of the stories of family history…that they didn't have just one more chance to build lasting memories.

After our loved ones have gone home to be with the Lord, we will never again have the opportunity to do all those things we wished we would have done while they are alive. That's why I encourage you to take the time now to enjoy those you love.

Don't Wait…Start Now!

Many times, we have thoughts of our legacy and what we are leaving behind. However, way too often those thoughts are just that—thoughts. Most people don't act on those thoughts until it is too late. I encourage you to sit down and take the time to purposefully create something for the people you love and care about.

You don't have to spend a lot of money—a simple phone call or visit will create new memories. The most important thing to remember is to spend time with the ones you love as much as you can. Don't let the busyness of everyday life stop you from being with the people you love most.

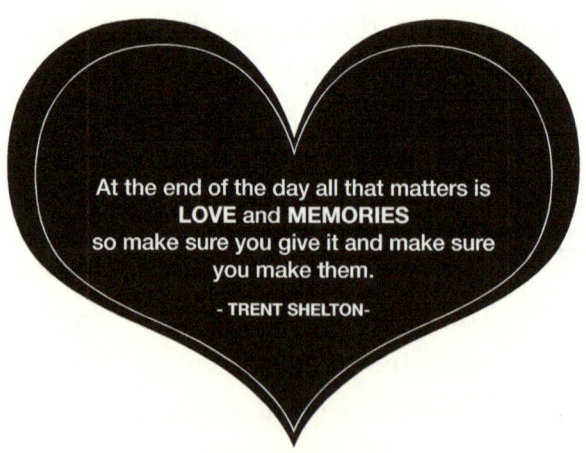

At the end of the day all that matters is **LOVE** and **MEMORIES** so make sure you give it and make sure you make them.

- TRENT SHELTON -

Creating a legacy and lasting memories is not about death and dying, it's about life

and living. It's about making connections and sharing precious moments with the special people in your life. It gives your loved ones something to hold on to. Your loved ones will have something that can provide healing and comfort year after year, and generation after generation. It's a reminder of who you were, what you loved, what was important to you and what contributions you made.

PART 2
The Homegoing Celebration

*"Birth is an Opportunity,
Life is a Blessing, and
Death is a Celebration."*

Andrew Mwangasa

First Things First

A *broken heart* is the **worst**, it's like having broken ribs Nobody can see it **but it hurts** every time you *breathe*

Losing someone you love is one of the most heartbreaking things you will ever experience. In this section, I am going to walk you through all of the details for your loved one's homegoing celebration. It's the same process I take my families through at Hadley Davis. But, before we get into that, there is something else we need to talk about first - your emotional and mental well-being.

Being a funeral director means more to me than just preparing a body or directing a funeral service. This is my life. I eat, sleep, and breathe it every day. I have a passion for the funeral industry that cannot be adequately expressed in words. It is my calling and I strive to be better every day—not just for myself, but also for those I serve.

Every person that walks into Hadley Davis becomes a part of our family. The very first thing I do when a grieving family member

arrives is to give each one a hug. If they need to cry, I let them cry. If they need to vent a little, I let them do that, too.

I am a counselor. I am a friend. I am a source of support and encouragement. One of the first things I tell my families is that it is okay to grieve. That's why I have this advice for you...

Understand that everyone deals with death differently.

As you are interacting with your family and other loved ones during this time, be patient--not only with them but with yourself, too. Know that it is completely okay for you to feel or think the way you do. Don't try to hide or censor your emotions.

Let yourself be vulnerable.

Some people try to be strong for everyone

else so that they don't appear weak or vulnerable. They don't want others to worry about them. I've seen people isolate themselves and have emotional breakdowns as they suffered alone in pain.

Remember, family support is a give and take. It is great for you to be there for others, but you should also let others be there for you.

> "Grief is **NOT** a disorder, a disease or sign of weakness. It is an emotional, physical and spiritual **necessity**, the price you pay **FOR LOVE** The only cure for grief is to **grieve**"
>
> - Earl Grollman -

Allow others to help you.

If you are the kind of person who is uncomfortable asking for help, I understand. Many of us are so used to doing everything for everyone else that we feel strange allowing others to do things for us. However, this is not the time to let your pride get in the way.

When you are overwhelmed with grief and stress, it is wonderful to know there are people who have your back. But you will never know it if you don't let them in.

Refuse to fight with your family members.

When you're grieving it is very easy to lash out at others. Your emotions are on edge and super sensitive to every little thing. Add to that the stress of trying to make sure you are honoring your loved one in the best way, and you've got a powder keg ready to explode.

Be patient with your family members and others helping you to plan the funeral services. Allow this to be a time to bring you closer together Instead of tearing you apart. You've already lost one loved one, you don't want to lose more because of minor disagreements.

Cherish the happy memories.

I have had people tell me all they can think about is their loved one dying. Especially if the loved one was sick for a long time, they play over and over in their minds scenes of their family member in the hospital. It breaks their heart every time they think of their loved one, so they try to forget.

I encourage my families to keep the memories of their loved one alive. Remember the time you spent together, the lessons they taught you, and how much they added to your life.

When you keep these words of advice in mind, the process of grieving your loved one will be a little bit easier. Remember this, the pain of death may never go away but, with God's help, you can learn to live through it.

Choosing The Right Funeral Home

Trust in the LORD with all your *heart,* and lean not on your own understanding In all your ways acknowledge Him, & He will direct your *paths*

Proverbs 3:5-6

If your loved one did not make arrangements prior to death, it will be up to you and other family members to choose the funeral home and make the arrangements.

In the past, most people would select a funeral home based on family tradition. However, many of the older family owned funeral homes are no longer in existence and there are so many new ones popping up. There are a lot of options to choose from, so you must be careful.

Many people have been taken advantage of by funeral homes when they are facing one of the most difficult times in their lives—it is horrific. I find it appalling that during grief, a time when they should be loved and cared for, is when vultures prey on them the most. For instance, if you have insurance, they make you feel as if some items are necessary when they are really not. They want to use up every single dollar in your insurance policy.

Money is not solely for the grave or cemetery. Educating yourself is the best way to

avoid this. Shop around and compare prices. Make sure to know what services are being provided for the money you are spending. Get all of this in writing before you present any information about your insurance policies to the funeral director.

I mentioned earlier about the pop-up funeral homes owned by unlicensed, uneducated individuals who are only in the funeral industry to make a quick buck. They do not have a heart for service.

When these funeral homes open, they have very high overhead expenses. These high expenses are passed on to the families with overpriced services. Because they want to make a lot of money quickly, they treat your loved ones like they are on an assembly line instead of handling them with dignity and care.

Do Your Homework

Would you have surgery from a doctor who was not licensed or educated? When you have a medical issue, would you just pick any doctor without finding out as much about them as possible? Of course not.

The same kind of care should be taken when you are choosing a funeral home for your loved one. When selecting a funeral home, it is very important for you to choose one that is qualified to meet your particular needs.

The main questions you want to ask yourself are:

- Have I visited this funeral home?

- Have I ever attended a service directed by this funeral home?

- Am I comfortable with this funeral home?

- Do I feel the funeral director understands my needs and is committed to helping me achieve my vision?

- Does the funeral home offer all the services I want?

- Does the funeral home offer affordable prices?

- Does the funeral director understand my religious or cultural needs?

Shop Around

      Contrary to popular belief, the prices at all funeral homes are not the same. Some funeral homes even fluctuate from one service to the next

      One of my biggest battles when I first opened Hadley Davis was when I displayed the prices for our services right on the marquee out front. I want my potential clients know exactly

what to expect when are comparing funeral prices.

The other funeral home owners in the area were not at all pleased with this. Not only was I sharing upfront prices but in most cases my prices were way lower than theirs. In all cases, the quality of my services far exceeded everyone else's. I kept my prices low and my quality high to help people and let them know they can have elegant and professional services without losing everything.

If you are price conscious, I recommend you do a little research before you select the funeral home you will use. Again, I must warn you to be careful! Some funeral homes will go lower on their prices to attract you to do business with them, but they don't deliver what they promise. Don't just take their word for it. Check out their work and ask for referrals.

Determine your budget before you go to the funeral home.

DO NOT take your insurance policy to the funeral home and just hand it over. That's a sure-fire way to get ripped off. It is sad but there are people who will preay on you at your weakest time. They will set their prices based on the amount of a family's level of insurance coverage. They will either raise their prices or add additional services they don't need, which is utterly shameful.

That is something I've been fighting against since the very beginning of my career in the funeral industry. Before I will even allow a family to tell me about the insurance they have, we talk about what they need. Many times, I will even suggest a more practical and less expensive option for a family instead of trying to get them to choose expensive services they don't need. I

remind my families that they still have to live after the funeral.

 My advice to you is to consult with your family before you go to the funeral home. Tell the funeral director what your budget is and stick to it.

Meeting With The Funeral Director

    Visiting the funeral home to arrange your loved one's funeral services is often a quite stressful experience. Not only are you emotionally affected by their death, you're anxious about making the right decisions. On top of all that, it's likely you have no idea what to expect when you arrive at the funeral home. So, let's talk about that for a bit.

    I can't speak for other funeral homes, but I am going to share with you what happens when a family walks into Hadley Davis. We strive for the very best experience for our families and pray that no matter the funeral home you visit, you will have a similar experience wherever you go.

What Happens On Your First Visit To The Funeral Home

- As soon as you walk through the front door, you will be greeted warmly by members of our team —with smiles, hugs, and words of comfort.

- You will be asked a few preliminary questions and then be immediately taken to the funeral director's office.

- Before the funeral arrangement conversation goes very far, you will be given a copy of our General Price List, Casket

Price List, and any other appropriate price-related documents. This is done to ensure compliance with the Federal Trade Commission's Funeral Rule.

- The funeral director will then ask you some questions about the deceased such as name, birth date, death date, next of kin, and other biographical details to complete the relevant paperwork.

- We will then discuss your wishes and help you to come to a decision about the plans for the funeral, memorial service, or celebration-of-life

Paperwork & Documentation

Accuracy is very important when you are completing the death paperwork, and writing a detailed obituary, So, when it comes to the task of sharing your loved one's biographical details,

you'll want to bring as much documentation of the following as possible:

- The deceased's full name
- Their Social Security number
- Parents' names
- Spouse and children's names
- Maiden name of mother
- Marital status
- Educational history
- History of military service
- Work history
- Hobbies and interests
- Church affiliation
- A list of organizational and club memberships
- A recent photograph

Naturally, if you're unable to bring any of this information, you can always provide it later.

Planning for the Funeral Event

The second step in the funeral arrangement conference is to plan a meaningful ceremony to pay tribute and celebrate the life of your loved one. This is really at the heart of what you'll be doing when you meet with the funeral director. In order to facilitate things, we ask our families to bring:

- Pre-arrangement papers, if applicable
- Clothes in which to bury or cremate your loved one
- Cemetery property information, if applicable
- A list of preferred charities for memorial donations, if applicable
- A list of pallbearers, if applicable
- Desired musical and readings selections

In addition to those standard items, you should also bring your warm memories and

heartfelt desire to honor your loved one. After all, you will be planning your loved one's funeral, memorial service, or celebration of life and your stories, personal perceptions, and insights will help to enhance the service by adding elements of their character and lifestyle.

Keep This in Mind...

Your first visit to the funeral home can be very intense and emotionally draining. You should be among people who really care about your welfare. You need to be supported throughout the funeral arrangement process, in any way you need.

Who Can Make Decisions?

To make decisions regarding your loved one's funeral services, you must be considered as a "next of kin". In order to qualify as next of kin, a person must be over 18 years old. The relationships listed below usually apply

to biological, adoptive, half, and step relations equally.

- Spouse/domestic partner
- Children
- Parents
- Siblings
- Authorized guardian
- Grandchildren
- Great-grandchildren
- Nieces and nephews
- Grand-nieces and grand-nephews
- Grandparents
- Aunts and uncles
- First cousins
- Great-grandchildren of Grandparents
- Second cousins
- Fiduciary (a legally appointed trustee)

Funeral Etiquette

THERE ARE SOME THINGS THAT MONEY CAN'T BUY....
LIKE MANNERS, MORALS AND INTEGRITY.

Before we end this section, there is one last thing to discuss—funeral etiquette.

Over the past decade or so, I have seen a lot of changes in the way people show up and behave at funeral services--and it hasn't been a change for the better.

There was a time when funeral services were attended with reverence and respect. Men wore suits. Women wore dresses. Everyone behaved with decency and decorum The homegoing celebration was one occasion when people were on their best behavior.

Not anymore.

Quite frankly, I am appalled by some of the things I see these days at funeral services. It's as if people no longer respect the memories of their loved ones. What used to be held in high regard is now treated with indifference.

It breaks my heart to see how much things have changed. That's why I do my best

to counsel and advise my families on the basics of funeral etiquette. It is so important for us to understand that a funeral service is a sacred and holy event. We are not only celebrating the life of a loved one, we are also honoring the transition of their spirit to their heavenly home.

Funeral Attire

Dark colors are no longer the required norm for funerals. Instead of black or gray, many people choose to wear a variety of colors. Some families choose to wear white to signify the holiness of their loved one's transformation to be with the Lord. Other families choose to wear the loved one's favorite color. Some families create special t-shirts or other memorabilia to honor the deceased. All of that is acceptable. It's not the color that makes a person's funeral attire respectful—it's the condition and appearance of that attire.

For example, I've seen men wearing sagging, torn pants and women wearing low-cut, short dresses that reveal way too much. A funeral service is not a cook out at the park or a night at the club. Even if the service is not held in a church, there is still a level of propriety that should be maintained.

Your funeral attire should reflect the seriousness of the occasion. At the very least, it should be clean, pressed, and neat. If there is a question about whether or not something is appropriate to wear to a funeral, ask yourself, "Would I wear this to church or to a job interview?"

Attending the Funeral Service

A funeral is a serious and sacred occasion. I know I've said that quite a few times already, but I feel it is so important to keep reminding you

of that. You would be surprised at how many people choose to forget this truth.

They demonstrate this by the way they show up. Not only in their attire but also in the way they behave. For example, many people are more respectful to others in a movie theater than they are to others at a funeral service. Talking loudly, arriving late, taking pictures or videos are things people refrain from doing during a movie but have no problem doing at a funeral service.

I am not going to give you a long list of dos and don'ts here because there is only one simple thing to keep in mind—funeral etiquette is all about respect. Respect for your deceased loved one's memory. Respect for the seriousness of the occasion. Respect for your other family members and friends.

What's Next?

LIFE IS TOUGH

You just have to learn to take it day to day and have faith that in the end, everything is going to be Okay.

After the homegoing celebration, families often ask us, "What's next?" They have lots of questions and wonder how to handle all of the legal, financial, and emotional concerns.

For many people, the first weeks and

months following the funeral of a loved one are more difficult than the funeral home visitation or the funeral service. Friends and supporters have gone home. Life gets back to normal rather quickly for everyone else. But, for you, it seems as if the grieving has just started.

Your loved one's death continues to become more of a reality. And the very thought of facing your life over the next few weeks and months fills you both with loneliness and a sense of dread. It all feels like way too much to deal with, and I want you to know that right now it's okay to take it slowly.

You'll be faced with strong emotions. Sometimes you won't be able to sleep through the night. And, through all of this, you will still have to cope with daily life and also be responsible for taking care of many details related to your loved one's estate.

> Always defend your right to heal at your own pace. You are taking your time. You are allowed to take your time.

    Immediately after the funeral service, you should give yourself lots off time to rest. Even if you find that you can't sleep all the way through the night, you can always just lie down and shut your eyes for a time. Especially when you are

feeling overwhelmed with emotions and grief, taking some quiet time can help you relieve the stress. Do your best to calm your mind by praying and listening to inspirational music and messages. And, when you have to do difficult things like handle your loved one's estate, never hesitate to call upon a friend or family member to help.

There are no one size fits all solutions.

Everyone's circumstances are different, and each person grieves differently. However, I have some tips that can help you cope and get through this tough time.

Stay connected to your loved one.

First, there is no reason for your relationship with the person who has died to end. Death ends a life, but it doesn't end a relationship. If you are used to sharing your day

with the person who has died or calling them just to chat when something heavy is on your mind, then continue to do this. Many people continue to have conversations with the person who has died and although this may sound strange, it is less unnatural than being expected to abruptly end the relationship. If you are not comfortable with talking to someone you can no longer see or hear then write down what you want to say in a journal.

Forget "normal".

There is a new normal now. The way you behaved and felt before your loved one's passing is not how you may behave or think now. Whatever you are feeling, or thinking is actually probably quite normal considering the unusual set of circumstances. Emotions or lack of emotions, sleeplessness, a constant sense of unreality, and of course a feeling of guilt, which

never fails to raise its ugly head. Whatever your thoughts and feelings it is important to know that they are probably quite natural.

Let the tears flow.

Crying is the body's very clever way of reducing stress and a very natural reaction. It doesn't matter whether it is days, weeks, months or years after the death, if you feel like having a good cry don't question it, just allow it. Your body is telling you that you need the release. Suppressing tears in the long term is not a healthy option. The same applies if you are supporting someone else in their grieving process: it is important to allow them to cry and not try and 'cheer them up'.

Finally, know that you will not always feel as bad as you do now. Getting through each day after a death may feel like a challenge, but

by focusing more and more on today and less on yesterday you will make progress. There will be good days and bad days but in time you will find that the good days outweigh the bad. The landscape of your life may have changed dramatically but the changes will slowly start to feel more familiar and one morning you will wake up with the knowledge that you are now able to see beyond tomorrow.

My Prayer for You

As I wrote this book, my mind was focused on you. God placed the vision for this book on my heart and He showed me there is a great need and purpose for what I have shared in these pages.

All around me I see the devastating effects of people being taken advantage of during a time when they should be loved on and supported most. When I took the vow to uphold the standards of integrity and excellence in the funeral industry, I made a commitment to be a beacon of light in the funeral industry. My life as a licensed funeral director and funeral home owner is more than just about business. It is in my heart to serve. This is the work I do to honor others and most importantly to honor God.

I pray this book opened your eyes and

gave you keen insights into the funeral industry. I also pray that after reading this book you are now more prepared to get through life's most difficult time.

    My prayers will continue to be with you and yours. May God richly bless you.

    Until we meet again,

Lori Hadley Davis

Words of Comfort & Encouragement

    Grieving can be the most difficult time for people. Trying to balance the feelings of pain and loss while going forward with your everyday life. With this collection of bible verses and words of inspiration, we can turn to God's word for ease and comfort as we look to overcoming grief.

He will wipe every tear from their eyes. There will be no more death or mourning or crying or pain, for the old order of things has passed away.

- Revelation 21:4 -

....

The LORD is close to the brokenhearted and saves those who are crushed in spirit.

- Psalm 34:18 -

....

He heals the brokenhearted and binds up their wounds.

- Psalm 147:3 -

....

My flesh and my heart may fail, but God is the strength of my heart and my portion forever.

- Psalm 73:26 -

"Then you shall call and the Lord will answer; you shall cry and he will say Here I am."

Isaiah 58.9

Surely, he took up our pain and bore our suffering, yet we considered him punished by God, stricken by him, and afflicted. But he was pierced for our transgressions, he was crushed for our iniquities; the punishment that brought us peace was on him, and by his wounds we are healed. We all, like sheep, have gone astray, each of us has turned to our own way; and the LORD has laid on him the iniquity of us all.

- Isaiah 53:4-6 -

....

Have I not commanded you? Be strong and courageous. Do not be afraid; do not be discouraged, for the LORD your God will be with you wherever you go.

-Joshua 1:9 -

And we know that in all things God works for the good of those who love him, who have been called according to his purpose.

- Roman's 8:28 -

....

Blessed are those who mourn, for they will be comforted.

- Matthew 5:4 -

....

You are now very sad. But later I will see you, and you will be so happy that no one will be able to change the way you feel.

- John 16:22 -

There is no way around grief only through. Know that you are in the *hands of God* and you are never alone

— Mary Davis

May God, the source of hope, fill you with all joy and peace by means of your faith in him, so that your hope will continue to grow by the power of the Holy Spirit.
- Romans 15:13 -

....

Blessed be the God and Father of our Lord Jesus Christ, the Father of mercies and God of all comfort, who comforts us in all our tribulation, that we may be able to comfort those who are in any trouble.
- 2 Corinthians 1:3, 4 -

....

Fear not, for I am with you; be not dismayed, for I am your God. I will strengthen you, yes, I will help you, I will uphold you with My righteous right hand.
- Isaiah 41:10 -

About The Author

Lori Hadley Davis

Lori Hadley Davis is a dynamic motivational speaker, inspirational author and

successful entrepreneur who empowers men and women to eliminate excuses and exercise faith to get from where they are to where they really want to be.

Lori is the visionary and founder of the Hadley Davis Funeral Corporation. From an early age, she had a burning desire to become a Funeral Director which led her to pursue and successfully graduate with a degree from Miami Dade College. Faced with resistance, rejection and tragedy along her journey, Lori overcame all obstacles with great leaps of faith and determination. Lori is now the proud owner of Hadley Davis Funeral Home in Liberty City and Miami Gardens.

Lori is passionate about educating, encouraging and empowering people through the process when dealing with the loss of a loved

one. She has helped hundreds of people strive through stressful situations and triumph over tragedy- always reminding them that no matter what, - she loves them and so does God.

One of Lori's biggest pet peeves about the funeral industry is the way aspiring funeral directors are being trained. They are only instructed on the protocol and procedures of the funeral industry. Lori's dream is to teach and train upcoming students and directors in the funeral industry—not just on the standards and rules but also on the true efficacy of being a funeral director. To that end, Lori is currently studying to earn a Bachelors, and ultimately a Masters, degree in business.

Lori is well known in her community for her service and charity. She isn't afraid to get down and dirty with the people to make a

difference. She also is an online influencer and has made a great impact amongst thousands on social media, inspiring people to push past their pain, be their best and to go after their dreams. Lori believes, your best is on the inside of you so if you want it, you can have it. Put God first, have faith and continue to press forward knowing that your determination has to be greater than your expectation.

     Lori is a wife and mother of three children and grandmother of seven grandchildren, residing in Miramar, Florida.

Notes

Use this section to keep track of your planning and have all of the details in one handy place.

www.ingramcontent.com/pod-product-compliance
Lightning Source LLC
Chambersburg PA
CBHW060454080526
44584CB00015B/1435